THE ZIG ZAG WOMAN

MAGGIE SAWKINS

TWO RAVENS
PRESS

Published by Two Ravens Press Ltd
Green Willow Croft
Rhiroy
Lochbroom
Ullapool
Ross-shire IV23 2SF

www.tworavenspress.com

The right of Maggie Sawkins to be identified as author of
this work has been asserted by her in accordance with the
Copyright, Designs and Patent Act, 1988.
© Maggie Sawkins, 2007.

ISBN: 978-1-906120-08-5

British Library Cataloguing in Publication Data. A CIP record
for this book can be obtained from the British Library.

Designed and typeset in Sabon by Two Ravens Press.
Cover design by David Knowles and Sharon Blackie.

Printed on Forest Stewardship Council-accredited paper by
Biddles Ltd., King's Lynn, Norfolk.

This book is printed on paper made
from fully managed and sustained
forest sources.

FSC

TT-COC-002303

© 1996 Forest Stewardship Council A.C.

About the Author

Maggie Sawkins was born in 1953 and spent her childhood in Leigh Park, a large council housing estate north of Portsmouth. She began writing poetry at the age of nine after being inspired by her head teacher. Her first poems were published in *Hampshire Poets* when she was seventeen. After a series of office jobs, including three years with *The Exeter Flying Post,* Maggie returned to education and went on to gain an MA with distinction in Creative Writing. For the past twelve years she has taught students with specific learning difficulties at South Downs College near Portsmouth.

In 2004, Maggie co-founded the popular Tongues & Grooves Poetry and Music Club in Southsea where she now lives with her husband, younger daughter and a growing menagerie. Flarestack published a pamphlet collection, *Charcot's Pet*, in 2003. *The Zig Zag Woman* is her first full collection.

Acknowledgements

I would like to thank the editors of the following publications in which poems, or earlier versions of these poems, have appeared:

Acumen, Coal City Review (University of Kansas), Dreaming Beasts Anthology, Four Caves of the Heart Anthology, Images of Women Anthology, Iota, Lapidus, Magma, Mouth Ogres, Mslexia, Obsessed with Pipework, Pendulum, Quattrocento, Seam, Smiths Knoll, The Book of Hopes and Dreams, Spokes, Sussex Seams Volume 2, The Interpreter's House, Writing Women.

The Birds won first prize at The Annual Writers' Conference in 1998 and was featured as *The Weekend Poem* on BBC Knowledge in 2001. *The Mummy* won first prize at The Annual Writers' Conference in 1999. *Brass Monkeys* and *Bronzefield* were commended in Second Light Poetry Competitions. *The Zoo Keeper's Song* won the Poetry Poster Competition at the 8th Poetry Plus Festival, Croydon.

I would like to thank all those who have given me encouragement, but especially: Brian Daldorph, Graham Fawcett, Vicki Feaver, Wendy French, Katherine Gallagher, Ed Hurd, Charles Johnson, John Killick, George Marsh, Stephanie Norgate, Myra Schneider and Dilys Wood. Thanks also to my family, past and present, for putting up with the silence.

Introduction

The first section of this collection contains poems about my childhood and how it was influenced by my parents' past. The title, *The Little Box Remembers Her Childhood,* is borrowed from Vasko Popa's poem, *The Little Box.* The poems, written over the last thirteen years, are arranged so that they tell the story of my life – though this wasn't a conscious intention in their writing. The earliest one, *Into the Silence,* begins with a memory of myself as a baby in my father's arms. Something that concerns me is the difficulty of breaking away from the weight of the past – what Larkin called 'the coastal shelf.' I've noticed that even when I try to write upbeat poems, a little bit of the darkness manages to slip through! I think poems are like dreams – they know more than you do.

The middle section entitled *My Mutant Butterfly* has poems about my elder daughter who was diagnosed with a serious mental illness in 2001. At the time I was studying for an MA in creative writing and I found it useless trying to write about anything else. The last section is a kind of 'coming through' – with themes of displacement, acceptance and an opening-up to wider issues.

The title of the collection comes from the 'Zig-Zag Girl' illusion – a trick where the magician divides his assistant into thirds so that her middle appears to be displaced to one side. Sometimes in life you have to displace your heart in order to survive. Writing helps you to make sense of the past and the present – even if the subject matter is disturbing, the act of creation is positive – art allows you to find resolutions that can't be found in life.

Maggie Sawkins
Portsmouth 2007

For Catherine, Faith and Elliot

If we choose, we can live in a world of comforting illusion.

Noam Chomsky

Contents

The Little Box Remembers Her Childhood

Translations of the Silence

My Mutant Butterfly

Cuckoo

The Art of Detachment

The Little Box Remembers Her Childhood

Further Adventures of the Little Box

(in memory of The Little Box *by Vasko Popa)*

Dear Mr Popa

Since you are dead I am writing
with news of *The Little Box*.

When we first met (as a preface to a book
on how to cobble up a poem) it was like
looking into the face of a smile.

In July *The Little Box* and I attended
an event at The Botanical Gardens.
Though we were placed between lines
from *Paradise Lost* and *The Song of Quoodle*,
and the wind made the microphone groan
and the paper shake, you'll be pleased
to hear we held our own.

After, as we sat back on the grass,
and *Naming of Parts* boomed through
the speakers, people came up to ask
about *The Little Box*. I explained
I didn't know what it meant only that
it made me smile.

Then yesterday this:

after a brainstorm brought nil response
from my session with the mentally ill,
I took out *The Little Box* and sifted
its emptiness into the silence.

When I looked up your words were resting
like butterflies along their shoulders,
and on each face was a smile.

Sleep tight, Mr Popa;
I'm taking good care of *The Little Box*.

Into the Silence

My brother runs
round and round
howls like a Red Indian

you sit on the green
medicine cabinet
me in your arms

you pat my back
with your tattooed hand
twizzle my toes.

     ✦

In the backyard
yellow light shines
like a roman candle

from the kitchen window.
I hold on tight
to the fold

of your soft flannel trousers
as you lean towards
the blue touch paper.

     ✦

The nurse at the hospital
has the same name as me.
The bed smells of rubber.

She lifts a piece of gauze
with tweezers from a dish
shaped like the moon.

Underneath the white patch
my skin wrinkles
like brown crepe paper.

     ✦

3

The roast beef
ready to be carved
steam whorls snakelike

from vegetables
on the stove.
We cower in the corner

watch the knife rise in your hand
words spit from your mouth
We eat in silence.

◆

Saturday night
toasting bread
by the open fire.

As he turns to go
she throws her wedding ring
into the orange flames.

It lays till morning
swaddled in a halo of ash
in the cooling grate.

◆

He ate red ants
in Burma in the war
he told us

his back was pitted
from sleeping
on a bed of nails.

The other woman's daughter
found him.
His lips were blue.

Snake

He had it done on a whim
he told us, just before his spell
in Doolally.

Home from the war
he lived with the regret –
no matter that we loved it.

Days at the beach he'd sit
with his shirt on, or lie forever,
his back to the sand.

It was a work of art
that began at his waist
and wound its way up

around the trunk
of a palm tree and ended
where we could see

its blue arrow tongue
flickering at the nape
of his neck.

Brass Monkeys

My mother's dusters flap –
tiny yellow sails above the cabbages.
Inside everything sparkles

like a wedding ring dipped in vinegar.
Ginger cat hairs, angel cake crumbs
the family's fingernails banished into thin air.

Bring in the washing!
Next door's mongrel's on the loose.
Pegs are flying.

Jesus, Mary and Joseph! Fetch the broom!
Too late. The tail of Dad's shirt's
wrapped round its rubbery tongue.

What's skin made of?
I'm staring into the pink ear
of my baby rabbit.

Before anyone can answer
it's leapt from my lap
into a wigwam of sweet peas.

Faster than a blue-arsed fly,
she told Dad later
over Vesta chop suey and rice.

It's not fair! Just as the princess falls
in love with the genie, I'm packed off to bed.
Neither is a black man's bum, says Dad

as he tucks me up in stiff white sheets.
All night the drone of voices drifts through
the floorboards stinging my ears like bees.

The Birds

She got used to the birds
flying around the house

except for the days
when their cawing filtered
through the floorboards

and even the dog was afraid.

When friends or relations came
the birds disappeared through the windows
and waited on the roof top
or under the eaves.

One day the cawing stopped.

The birds settled in the silence
like a big black cloud.

In her bedroom she built a cage
and the birds flew in
one by one.

Weeks later she returned from school
found her mother and father
in the kitchen – kissing.

From her room she could hear
the flutter of a million tiny wings.

The door opened and the birds
glided through the house

weightless and blue.

Celery Soup

I fetch the chair from the Formica table
reach into the cupboard

take the butterfly opener
from the drawer
turn and turn till the ragged edge lifts.

The creamy liquid plops into the pan
I stir in a figure of eight
the way she taught me to.

I lay the tray with salt and pepper
arrange triangles of sliced white bread.

I carry it up to her room
where she's propped against the pillow,
steam warms her face but she doesn't smile

because every Friday they burn her skin
and they've taken her breast away.

It feels like a dream
except my footprints
are still there

embedded in the blueness
of a blue kitchen chair.

The Mummy

And one day my father moved
into my bed.

When he was at work
I'd go into my old room

sit on the candlewick spread
and inspect the tiny brown bottles

he'd left across my swan-head doily
on top of the orange box.

I'd lift up the tin-tacked curtain
and finger his letters and books.

At night he'd deliver me
to their big double bed

tuck me in tight and tight and tight

In the lamplight I'd stare
at the darkening ceiling

warm and wrapped
as a mummy.

9

After Dostoevsky

Since she's discovered Raskolnikov
she's dug a hole in the garden
to bury her school uniform
her flat black shoes.

She's acquired too
a taste for Smirnoff
and perfected the art of gesticulation.

And no-one has noticed –
her mother's busy in the kitchen
chopping parsnip and swede
and her father's flat out
in the potting shed.

Only the pawnbroker's boxer dog
sits up and growls as she swishes past
in her surplus store raincoat. An axe
tucked neatly under her arm.

The Back Room

After he left we painted the room
that was always too cold sit in, orange.

With my pocket money I bought a poster
a black and white abstract – hung it on the wall.

That Christmas we carried the table in –
set three places instead of four.

Above the blue heat of the paraffin stove
the picture swayed on its thin black strip.

I couldn't eat – all I could see was the space
between the fractured masts of a shipwreck.

Pink Salmon

In his manic phase
my father stole tins of pink salmon
for his cat.

Sometimes
he'd come round
with a bag full of bacon joints

and offer one to me
as if he was doing me a favour –
most times I'd say no.

Once, I must've said yes.
I was a single parent
with an empty fridge.

The joint stayed in there
so long it turned
silvery blue.

Such a Smallness

Such smallness
to remember –

the tiny silver cup
you made

out of the foil
from your pack

of Weights
as I watched

from your lap –
how you

crumpled it
threw it away.

I wanted to keep it
but didn't ask.

Since You Are Dead

I hope wherever you are
the weather's fine and you no longer feel
the need to wear your trilby hat.
You'll be pleased to hear
I'm writing this in the garden of a retreat
and I'm happy now, surrounded by peonies
just like the ones we had at home, and by the way,
I passed my degree with colours.
But what I really should say
is even though I didn't cry at your funeral,
driving back from the hospital that day,
after reading to you from the *Comrade's Page*
of *The Burma Star*, and wishing the gravy
on your shirt wasn't there,
nor the scar on your forehead,
I'm pretty sure when I stopped
at the traffic lights near your flat,
the colours blurred from red to green
and from green to red.

Ever After

And one day I'll invite them to tea.
I'll make salmon fishcakes
with lemon and parsley

arrange slices of tomato
on a dish shaped like the moon.

I'll drape the table with lace
and light a candle.

My mother will arrive in her lilac dress
and soft red shoes.

On her arm will be my father
in his trilby hat. For once
he'll lift it off. I'll kiss his head

and he'll tell the tale
of the bald-headed donkey.

We'll sit down to eat
and my brother and me will promise
not to argue over the tick-tock spoon.

While Toby curls and dreams in his basket
the clatter of knives and forks
will fill the room.

Sophie the cat will jump to the table
and swipe a piece of fishcake
from my father's fork.

For a moment there'll be silence.

Then my mother will smile
and begin to laugh. Then
my brother, my father, and me.

And we'll laugh so loud
the neighbours will bang on the walls.
We'll stop and look at each other
there'll be sparks in our eyes.

And we'll start again
and the roof will fly
from the top of the house
and our laughter will fill the sky

will lighten our blood
will lighten our bones
will carry us up to a nest made of stars.

And that will be the end of the story.

Translations of the Silence

A Pair of Small Ears

I have come to translate the silence.
I've bought paper and pencils
and a pair of small ears.

I ask you
not to disturb me
until the task is done.

First I will unwrap the ears
and place them face up
on the floor.

You will observe their strangeness
these tiny shallows
these bridges of bone.

They are waiting for the sound
of no sound –
nothing is permitted

not even the intermittent
buzz of a fly nor the tick of a wall.

You must soften your breath
learn patience –
shuffle along any vagrant thought.

Soon the ears will begin
to quiver – gently they will
pick up the pencils at their side.

Listen closely –
the word is about to be
written.

Blight

It first appears as white fuzz
on the underside
of leaves.

Like an anger
that doesn't tell
it spreads to the stems

that blacken and wither
under the rainsplash
and wind-driven spores.

Then it falls
to the earth and buries itself
in the heart of the tuber

where it burrows and burrows
till all is black
all is rotten –

a sodden necrosis.
And then
there is no heart.

Migration

In her seventy-seventh year
she told me her secret
as we said our goodbyes

at the front door
of her council high rise
a white moth circled

the leaded glass lamp
hanging in the hallway
as I left her there

a child in a pale blue dress
tanned feet bare
hiding from her brother

in a Dunbeggan barn
too many safe houses away
from her father

heading blind
towards the harbour
of Boston Bay.

American Wake

At the boot-hollowed threshold
seventeen miles from Skibbereen
I listen for my grandfather's
by God I'll make you skip, boy
sing-song voice.

At the farmhouse table
where he might have planned
his American dream,
I trace the wood as if I could find
the whorl of his fingerprints
somewhere in the grain.
Then in a tin box I see
the photograph –
his flock of children left
to fend like babes in the wood.

And the tales my mother told me,
that once seemed as distant
as another planet,
flash the room – whiting her eyes
like lightning on a star starved night.

The Kitchen

where I find myself
back at the door
listening

to the thud thud of an iron
where if I push
a little more

I will see the shine
on the back
of her still black hair

and the sun gleaming
through gingham curtains
and as it's a bad day

our dog squeezed in between
the cooker
and the eggshell wall

where if I stay long enough
I will see her turn
her face creased

the pile of pillowcases
shirts sheets flung to the floor
and my own small face

and her fingers
pulling pulling
the roots of her hair.

Our Pet Mother

If only she would come down
from the mountain and be
like one of the chinchillas
Mr Chapman spent eleven years coaxing,
we would wrap her in iced black sheets
just like he did
until she got used to the sun.

Then we would build a cage
right here in our bedroom,
tempt her with titbits of roots,
alfalfa and bark,
give her a tray of white sand
to keep her cool.

Each night we'd promise
to lift up the latch,
let her hop onto the carpet
and watch as she ricocheted
from wall to wall.

Then we would catch her and cup her
in the palms of our hands,
sink our fingers
into her plush grey fur,
and feel her quiver. She'd be
so so soft we would almost drown.

Red Geranium on an Isolation Ward

She knew how to die –
the earth around her stem
was so dry it refused
the water we poured there

and though, like a ritual,
we snapped off
each bruised cluster
before it had time
         to fall,
     there was no renewal –

even the sun pushing
     its fist through the window
          could not coax her.

Mobile

cut out sheep
twirl in silence
first one way

then the other
models of obedience
they seem

to want for nothing
except perhaps
the gift of air

they have no need
to be watched
nor do they care

if I'm awake
or sleeping
and if the room

should go up in flames
they will blacken
into neverness

and won't have
to worry about anyone
missing them

or stare through
the window
into the rain.

Silence

It's not the kind that whips its tail
against the heart and makes you wonder
    what ill you've done;

not the kind that sets up home
between the ears or drones in the blood
until you no longer can hear the man
    on the radio or the cat's meow;

it's not the kind that broods well
into the night, so that even between
the sheets, the words you're trying to read
    lift from the page like a swarm –

it's not the kind whose off switch,
though so close, is out of reach –
    no, it's not that kind of silence.

My Mutant Butterfly

Stalkers

I join you on the edge
of your bed

      It's late but not yet

too late

the smoke from our cigarettes
        curls into a single cloud

I try to follow

    the thoughts that stalk you
        like Escher's grey men
           in his house of stairs

      You have seen them

        in waiting rooms
    and on TV quiz shows
in the park by the tropical bird house
sweeping leaves

In the dark

I will make my way home
I will ignore the trip-trap
of footsteps that follow

I will not turn my head.

Rogue Gene

For years they had me talking
making stories out of ink spots.
But when they found it
it wasn't in me at all.
   It was in my daughter.

When they caught her
she hadn't slept for weeks.
They found pieces of dreams
scrawled across her room –
on the flaps of air mail envelopes,
origami paper, old tissues, even the walls.

There were tales of arsonists,
and snake-tossing jugglers,
chimpanzees flying high
on a giant trapeze.

As they approached with their instruments
she stripped off her clothes
and fled like a goose
through the window
into the path of a passing car.

   When they found it,
it didn't look like her at all.
It had my father's pixilated eyes.
His darkened stare.

Bad Patch

I dab the red dust
spattered across
the white bonnet

from the house brick
you'd used to smash
my windscreen

and think of the force
that once beat beside me
faint as a breeze

tinkling through foil
strung across a row
of baby cabbages

Crossfire

It hasn't moved for months.
It knows its place – on top of the dresser
facing the door.

Arum Lily
    the Afrikaans have a name for you:

Varkblom
Pig's Ear

no wonder you poke out
your yellow tongue.

Calla Lily
one day you will be caught
    in our crossfire.

Someone will wrench you
from your terracotta pot
and hurl you to the floor.

Names will fly.
Fists flail.

My Little White Hood

I will remember you
mute and beautiful –
    bite my tongue.

The Bruise

        arrived a few days later
a bright yellow pansy
on my right arm,
        then it disappeared.
Eventually
I threw away the clump
        of hair.

        Now there's nothing
left to show –
no cause for alarm –
        except for something,
somewhere there's this:
a small persistence
        a faint hiss of tears.

Incident at Christmas

Since then she only visits
in dreams though we look for her
everywhere – even along
the tree-lined avenue

where the only witnesses were
the fairy lights that blinked
with stupid happiness
from almost every window.

But she's less than nowhere.
All that's left is to wait
just beyond the corner
our hearts in our pockets, ticking.

My Daughter's Habit

A month's respite doesn't stop the heart
tilting in the cradle at the knock,

the scene replayed before I open the door.
I know from her expression what it is

she wants, but still she asks, and I fetch,
like a dog, hand over the score,

notice once more the half-moon scar
on the bone of her cheek.

The night swallows her shadow,
catches my sigh as she walks away.

I lean a while against the door,
listen as the wind worries the trees,

smother the thought: to press
a pillow against my slipping heart.

Bronzefield

Sounds like a place that once
was torched
by the breath of a god,

but more likely it was built
on a field of corn,

this building with high red walls

where you've finally
been netted –
my mutant butterfly.

When I come to visit
they search my mouth.

The Visit

Today is the saddest
of places

a near deserted corridor
of an old hospital

where I find myself listening

for the footfall
of my father's shadow,

and meet instead this tall young man
in a blue satin dress

who doesn't notice my heart
as it stalls.

I catch his eye – he hurries on –

as if all his life
he's been late for the ball.

Date Unknown

I will walk up a path
policed by poplars
the sky will be cloudless and blue.

In my hand an empty suitcase
scented with lavender,
swinging.

A patient will skitter past
in raincoat and scarlet slippers
and I'll tip my head.

In front of a circle of lawn
and gothic fountain
will be a redbrick building

that could be a mansion but isn't.

She'll be leaning against
a glass doorway
with lightness in her hair

like a girl from a Hopper painting,
except she is smiling.

I will walk towards her,
take her bundle of clothes,
unbuckle her hands.

A doctor will appear
as if from nowhere to wish
her well.

As we turn to go faces will stare
from darkened windows,
flowers will curtsey

trees uproot themselves
sprout wings
and fly.

Hostage

Back in her room of red walls
and brittle honesty

water paints and sugar paper
idle in drawers.

The bamboo blind
that once shielded her

from her garden of peeping toms
is rolled up

now the windows open
to the gaze of stars.

If only I could believe
in the magic she no longer believes in

I would snuff out this madness
unhex the instance of its birth

I would bridle her
and lead her to rippleless water

I would will the gods
to make her drink.

New

I will haul you up
 from the mound
   of cards newspaper cuttings
milk teeth wrapped in cotton
 the name tag that held the weight
       of you

with the silver bird scissors
 snip into your eyes your nose
   your mouth your chin

feeding rocking cooing I will undo
 the hours unfurl your fingers
  from the twist

of my hair

 I will scatter you
    onto a sheet
     of white vellum

unwrap your gift for stealing

the show then I will reassemble
     every tiny piece of you

until you appear
 abstract frameless
  the same but not the same.

Cuckoo

Charcot's Pet

Before my voice disappeared
like a rabbit up a sleeve
I wanted to be a singer
in the Folies Bergère.

The doctor is a kind man
he keeps me warm,
he feeds me seed cake
and Assam tea.

> But sometimes he makes me crawl.
> *Pick up the crumbs*
> *my little goose.*

At night I lie beside him
more silent than a blade of grass.
I allow his cold fingertips
to circle my heart.

Tomorrow, he says,
I must rehearse for the show
in the auditorium of the Salpêtrière.
The doctors will love me!

He has made me a hat
of peacock feathers.
He has taught me to bark.

When he stares into my eyes
he can make me do anything

> But he can't make me sing.

Cuckoo

It's one o'clock
and I slip in beside him

smelling of honeysuckle
and dusted in pollen,

I know he's awake

he's picking pieces of bracken
out of my hair.

I long to tell him about the pansies
and their Pekinese faces

all about the mandrakes
and the Queen Anne's Lace,

but he doesn't speak –
he's pretending he doesn't care.

All the same – I think he knows

I've been out haunting
those wooded bedlams again.

Episode

1999 – the year you thought your son's harelip
was a sign – you went to Cornwall
to watch the eclipse.

You kissed me on the lips
the night before. The sky darkened.
I watched from the shore.

Eight years – and the formation
on your forehead has turned into
a permanent frown.

I never knew it could take so long to drown.

In His Absence

We are in the land
of swishing doors –
rehearsing our lines.

Men in batman capes
and lamb's tail hair
pass to and fro.

They have elegant voices.

> *We are gathered here today*
> *to decide*
> *the fate of a boy.*

Mother, father, barristers,
Judge Sparrow
      and me.

The world passes from one hand
to another.

It's a wonder
the floor doesn't collapse
with the weight of it.

The Blue Violinist

(after Chagall)

My son, with the soft mule eyes
who learnt to dance
before he could talk
who played kiss-chase with his shadow,
      floats above our town
on a blue painted chair
his violin snug beneath his chin –

above the market square
the Peskowatik Asylum
the synagogue
above the drone of our prayers.

No-one,
the butcher, the cantor, the doctor
not even the rabbi
can tell me why he is up there
nor if he will ever come down:

I have tried to call him
tempted him with herrings and cakes
and glazé pears
even thrown him a bouquet
from our rooftop
like a hopeful bride.

But he will not budge.

The birds that perch on his knee
listen, cockheaded, to the strains
of his bow.

The snow is coming.

With every passing nightfall
I watch him float
      a fraction higher.

Late Call

When he hears him call to his wife,
Sweetheart, it's for you,
something inside him stirs
like a dog aroused in its sleep
by the memory of a lost bone.

He imagines their sofa flung with cushions
a vase of flowers on an occasional table
(some wrong he thought he'd done?)
his lips brushing her blonde hair
as he passes the phone.

A few muffled words then to bed alone.
At the window raw stars gather.
He closes his eyes, shuts the door
to his heart, plugs his ears
against the room's soft moan.

Briar Rose

Just because I am silent
they think I am sleeping –
those men who come

on their delirious white horses
who think they can wake me
with a kiss.

But this is bliss
to feign the sleep of the dead
on my bed of damask and lace.

I am in love
with these silent walls
with the secret of my breathing.

What makes them think
I am a bed or roses?
My head is filled with thorns.

Armour

After you there is home
and a room that promises warmth
but there is no warmth –
there is a carriage clock
with hands that have halted
at just past midnight
and a fire whose artificial logs
know just what they are.

There is a bed in a room
that promises peace
but there is no peace –
there is a bulb that shines
sixty watts too strong
and a drawing by Matisse
of a woman sleeping
shielding her breasts with her arms.

Then there is sleep
and a moon that hangs
in the middle of nowhere
cradling a calm that cuts at dawn
swift as a knife
slicing through skin
that thought it had grown
plate-thick as an armadillo.

Subject

Like Lucien's nudes,
in the writing they've become beautiful,

these yews with their peaks hewn clean
that form an archless archway

in the coiffeured garden of Holland House.
They could be twin vases,

densely green and gently curving,
or headless women

whose dreams have been clipped
and swept away.

Under a Stone

Leaf,
you no longer know
what it means

to be a leaf under a stone.

You've got too used
to the cold slab weight of it.

Absence of light
has turned you
into a wafer of veins

a leafshadow.

One skipping day
a child will come
and kick away the stone.

For a moment
you will lie there,
afraid of your own lightness

afraid of what you've become,

dazed
by the suddenness
of a white winter sun.

The Art of Detachment

Act

Dear Heart

It's time to come down
from your stilts. I have the answer –

I've passed the audition – I am soon to become

The Zig Zag Woman!

Tomorrow you'll accompany me to the stage
where we'll stand tall

under the purple spotlight.

I promise not to close my eyes if you promise
not to waver –

nor must you miss a beat as the blades slide
through our torso

as The Mighty Almeiro jolts us apart.

Believe me – it will be easier
this way.

Just think – each night boxed beside me
peaceful as a cat

as I slip into sleep to the thrum
of your purr.

Warm wishes,
a friend.

The Art of Detachment

So what if it's lonely?
Now and again a shape
will turn itself in from the darkness
then close on its tail a name:
comet, kite, kangaroo.
Others will arrive
without even a suitcase:
guilt, joy, passion, shame.

They are temporary guests
to be sent packing
into the arms of a story,
to be cast away with a kiss.

Passenger

You travel with me
silent, unseen.

I've done my best
to forget you

busied my head
with Sartre, Zen

books of endless
poetry.

So why the need
to make me quiver?

I know you're there
waiting to pluck me

from the air
with your ungloved hand

as if I were no more
than a flake

of blackened
snow.

The Stick

The thing I picked from your ceramic bowl

      to represent my soul

the stick I thought was a bone

            being parched and white

splintered

      into an ounce of lightness

the kind of stick you could place on a river

            watch float away

that no-one would notice

         or throw into the air

      for a dog to catch and chew

or for another to carry off

            and bury

like a bone.

Kalima's Son

We could be forgiven for thinking
    they are part of a carnival – these women
        dressed in purple and lime, turquoise and pink

    for admiring how the colours
   complement their bitter brown skins
as they crouch on the red earth

of Jebil Mara Mountain
    arranging parched white sticks
        to light a fire

    against a night
   that doesn't yet know the limit
of darkness

that blindfolds itself into believing
    the crackled cries
        of a woman's child

    as he's thrown to the flames
   by a devil on horseback –
are only laughter.

Elimination

Although he came from the mountains
(this much I learnt)

he didn't understand
my words for snow.

I fluttered my fingers
in front of him

but he only saw
the wings of birds.

I led him to the window
wrapped myself in my arms

at the shivering sky
but he only stared.

It was slow and involved
the elimination

of sun, wind and rain
but we got there.

Sometimes I think of him
back at the border

I imagine his mountains
their fingers of shadow

the stutter of gunfire
the quietness of snow.

Valentine's Day
(Madrid 2004)

A chorus of candlelight
on the city street brings me
back to that day

at Atocha Station
and I'm asking you to confirm
what I think it means:

the man on the billboard,
his head inside the mouth
of a Venus Fly Trap,

underneath a strap-line
– *diselo con flores* –
branded in red.

Now flowers
slumped against debris
speak only of silence.

One Fine Morning

(July 22)

And it could have been ours –
the heart skipping out of bed
one fine morning.

The heart with the day singing in its ears,
reaching for its coat,
closing the door.

And it could have been ours –
the heart finding itself caught
with its toes on the starting line,
tricked into running
over fields, over fences, over stiles.

And it could have been ours –
the heart tripping over itself,
its face to the land,
deafened by its own hooves of thunder.

And it could have been ours –
the heart both less and more
than a grain of sand –
without doing anything really wrong,
the heart struck dumb, like a dog's,
one fine morning.

Winter Funeral

(i.m. Marie Anne Salmon 1980 – 2005)

You were there in the eyes
of the harnessed black horses

in the grace
of an early December sun

You were there in the glaze
of a winterberry

in the poise
of the blackbird's song.

The Unfinisheds

They were bright once
            sometimes still
                        we can see them shine
between a cleft
            in a cloud
                        or in the shattered mirror
of the sun
            riding bareback
                        on the sea
for a moment
            they are there
                        in that place
where
      the tide turns
                  or in the space between
two breaths
                  and then they return
      to settle their souls
                        to stay
again like that
            like small dark things
                        set in amber.

Poem Composed While Doing a Headstand

The fir cone I picked from a Corsican forest,

    carried across an ocean

        nestled between balls of socks,

has fallen from the grate and rests

    where it meets my gaze as I pose

upside down in my daily practice.

I notice how it makes the perfect mandala,

    its curved wooden petals

        its skirt of hearts,

    and in the moment after chanting

my thoughts thin and clear as tinsel

I wonder how, each year in the dim days

    before Christmas, I have the gall

to consider spraying it gold.

A Blade of Grass

insubstantial thing
weightless
almost

no boast
of a smell
soundless

its journey
from the centre
of it all

crawled over
trampled on
mown down

it's easy
to lose interest
in a blade of grass

though between
your finger
and thumb

it's a strand
of sharp green
ribbon

blessed
with a will
to grow and grow

Inside

If I lie long enough
on the grass

I'll realise the sky is
a ceiling of glass

the sunset's a streak
in my heart

clouds are my thoughts
falling apart

the world's a receptacle
for keeping me in

its doors are locked
its in a spin

but if it helps to keep
me sane

I'll believe in you
Mister

with your bottle of shine
your bottle of rain.

The Zoo Keeper's Song

I could watch them for hours
Esmeralda and Zola
strolling up and down
on legs as long as stilted circus clowns.
With my daily offerings
of lettuce, radish and grape
I enter the enclosure
run my hand over
the primitive patchwork skin,
watch how they flutter their eyelashes
like two actresses
in an old time movie.

When I come back
I want to be the leaves
on the tallest trees.
I want to be devoured
by those magnificent tongues.

Notes

Further Adventures of The Little Box
Vasko Popa's poem, *The Little Box,* cited in the preface to
Ted Hughes' *Poetry in the Making.*

Snake
Doolally – British Army slang, from the Deolali sanatorium,
Marashtra, India.

After Dostoevsky
Raskolnikov was the protagonist in Fyodor Dostoevsky's
novel, *Crime and Punishment.*

A Pair of Small Ears
Inspired by Charles Simic's quote, '*Poems are the translations
of the silence.*'

American Wake
The name given to the last night before desperate voyagers
left their home for America during the Irish famine years.

Our Pet Mother
Mathias Chapman was the man responsible for the capture
and domestication of the chinchilla.

Bronzefield
The name of a women's prison in Ashford, Middlesex.

Charcot's Pet
Jean-Martin Charcot, the first of the great European
theorists of hysteria, frequently staged 'shows' to members
of his neurological service at the Salpetrière Hospital.
Blanche Wittman, Charcot's pet hysteric, was one of the
main attractions.

Kalima's Son
Kalima – one of the women caught up in ethnic killings and rape in Kidinyir village, Darfur, Sudan, 2004.

Valentine's Day
Diselo con flores – say it with flowers.

One Fine Morning
Written with thoughts of Jean Charles de Menezes who was mistaken for a terrorist and shot on London's underground – with lines borrowed from Kafka's *The Trial*.

Poetry from Two Ravens Press

Castings
Mandy Haggith

A new collection of poems by Mandy Haggith, whose writing reflects her love for the land and her concern for the environment – not just in the North-West Highlands where she now lives on a woodland croft, but also in her travels around the world.

'The poetry here shows real clarity of eye marking the dialogues of nature in a place, be that place the lonely Scottish crofting area that is home, or the course of the River Kelvin through the Lowlands, or a Russian forest.' **Tom Leonard**
'Outstanding originality and quality. Impressive for its sharpness, sympathy and decisiveness...' **Alan Riach**

£8.99. ISBN 978-1-906120-01-6. Published April 2007.

Leaving the Nest
Dorothy Baird

A collection of poetry by Dorothy Baird that represents a woman's journey into adulthood, through childbirth and motherhood and then on, as her children grow up and she passes into menopause and beyond.

'Images, ideas and sounds fill eyes, ears, mouth and mind – and not just occasionally, but constantly. These pieces are the outpouring of a remarkable talent. They inhabit this universe in all its aspects: seasons, elements, animals, birds, land and sea. They are unobtrusively urgent, unashamed, and alive with longing lingering thoughts and feelings, with intensely personal experiences which Dorothy Baird has triumphantly universalised. They are an eloquent meditation on our lives, filled with the rich loam of humanity. In an increasingly ugly and unpredictable world, these poems are a reminder and an example of just how beautiful life can be.'
Christopher Rush

£8.99. ISBN 978-1-906120-06-1. Published July 2007.

In a Room Darkened
Kevin Williamson

A first poetry collection by the founder, publisher and editor of the renowned underground literary magazine *Rebel Inc,* a publication which helped launch writers such as Irvine Welsh, Alan Warner and John King into the public domain.

£8.99. ISBN 978-1-906120-07-8. Published October 2007.

Fiction from Two Ravens Press
Nightingale
Peter Dorward

On the second of August 1980, at 1pm, a bomb placed under a chair in the second class waiting room of the international railway station in Bologna exploded, resulting in the deaths of eighty-five people. Despite indictments and arrests, no convictions were ever secured...

'Nightingale *is a gripping and intelligent novel; it takes an unsentimental and vivid look at the lives of a small group of Italian terrorists and the naive Scottish musician who finds himself in their midst in Bologna in 1980. Full of authentic detail and texture,* Nightingale *is written with clarity and precision. Peter Dorward tells this tragic story with huge confidence and verve.'*
Kate Pullinger

£9.99. ISBN 978-1-906120-09-2. Published September 2007.

Love Letters from my Death-bed
Cynthia Rogerson

There's something very strange going on in Fairfax, California. Joe Johnson is on the hunt for dying people; the Snelling kids fester in a hippie backwater and pretend that they haven't just killed their grandfather; and Morag, multi-bigamist from the Scottish Highlands is diagnosed with terminal cancer by Manuel – who may or may not be a doctor. Cynthia Rogerson's second novel is a funny and life-affirming tale about the courage to love in the face of death.

'Witty, wise and on occasions laugh-aloud funny. A tonic for all those concerned with living more fully while we can.' **Andrew Greig**

£8.99. ISBN 978-1-906120-00-9. Published April 2007.

Parties
Tom Lappin

Gordon yearns for a little power; Richard wishes reality could match the romantic ideal of a perfect pop song; Grainne wants life to be a little more like Tolstoy. Beatrice looks on and tries to chronicle the disappointment of a generation measuring the years to the end of the century in parties.

Parties is a black comedy about young people getting older, and learning to be careful what they wish for, lest they end up finding it.

£9.99. ISBN 978-1-906120-11-5. Published October 2007.

Prince Rupert's Teardrop
Lisa Glass

The story of a damaged woman's relationship with her mother, a nonagenarian Armenian haunted by the genocide of her people by the Turkish Army early in the twentieth century. When her mother disappears, it is left to this most unreliable and unpredictable of daughters to try to find her, in this moving, lyrical and provocative work.

£9.99. ISBN 978-1-906120-15-3. Published November 2007.

Short Fiction from Two Ravens Press

Highland Views: a collection of stories by David Ross.
£7.99. ISBN 978-1-906120-05-4. Published April 2007.

Riptide: an anthology of new prose and poetry from the Highlands and Islands. Edited by Sharon Blackie & David Knowles.
£8.99. ISBN 978-1-906120-02-3. Published April 2007.

Types of Everlasting Rest: a collection of short stories by Scotsman-Orange Prize winner Clio Gray.
£8.99. ISBN 978-1-906120-04-7. Published July 2007.

For more information on these and other titles, and for extracts and author interviews, see our website.

Titles are available direct from the publisher at
www.tworavenspress.com
or from any good bookshop.